How to
Survive the Economic
Meltdown

How to
Survive the Economic Meltdown

Practical and Spiritual Strategies for You and Your Friends

Patrick Morley

Executive Editor: Daphne Mayer Keys
Editors: Stephanie Lopez and Jamie Smith
Cover and Interior Design: Cathleen Kwas

Published by Man in the Mirror Books
180 Wilshire Blvd.
Casselberry, FL 32707

www.maninthemirror.org

Dedication

To Tommy Boroughs
A great friend as well as a great lawyer.
Thanks for helping me survive my meltdown.

TABLE OF CONTENTS

INTRODUCTION

THIS IS A BOOK for anyone entangled in the economic meltdown.

Because of where I'm coming from (mentioned in Chapter One), while writing I pictured someone in crisis because they've been living by their own ideas and made mistakes. That may be you, or maybe you're an innocent bystander who got mugged. In either case, you will find tons of spiritual and practical survival strategies to help you get through this crisis. You can read the chapters in any order. May God encourage you and give you concrete direction in these pages.

Want to reach out to your friends? We're setting up a website, www.survivethemeltdown.org, where you'll find tons of free bonus resources—videos and video clips of me speaking on the meltdown, a guide to lead a small group, free articles, helpful links, endorsements, and special pricing to buy books in bulk. You can even leave a comment! And if you want to present, or have someone present, a seminar, speech, or sermon to your church or business group, you will find message transcripts, sermon ideas, speaker notes, listener outlines, graphics, and sample promotional materials. You can also arrange for a Man in the Mirror faculty to teach a seminar, or purchase a Meltdown Event Planning Kit.

One

YOU'RE GOING TO GET THROUGH THIS

P EOPLE ARE GETTING LAID OFF. Men can't find jobs. Companies are being forced to do layoffs. People are taking pay reductions. Bills are going unpaid. Budgets are getting slashed. Home values have plummeted. Savings accounts are rapidly being emptied out. Investments have gone up in smoke.

And that's just in my family.

Our nation and the world are in an economic meltdown of freakish proportions. How are you going to survive?

Maybe you've lost your job—or fear it. Maybe you've watched your investments or paycheck shrink. Perhaps your business is way off.

Or maybe you're "okay," but still worry how it's all going to turn out. Inevitably, you have family and friends struggling to make ends meet.

Much will be written in the days ahead about why this happened (humanly speaking), who is to blame, how to fix it, and when it will be over. However, this book will not touch on any of those topics. The purpose of this book is to show you how to personally survive and learn from the economic meltdown.

Where I'm Coming From

First, let's go back to 1986 when a scenario developed not unlike what we're seeing today—at least in the broad strokes. The economy was bloated with excessive consumption funded by overly easy credit with limited oversight. Greed was rampant.

In my line of work—commercial real estate development—we had banks pulling up to our front door and rolling in wheelbarrows full of money that I could borrow on "easy terms." Being foolish and naive, I was accepting it.

So every day for the next seven years, I woke up not knowing whether or not I would be forced into bankruptcy.

Because of the aggressive lending and—just so the blame gets shared equally—aggressive borrowing, the commercial real estate market was grossly overbuilt. Banks and Savings and Loan Associations were stretched thin. Businesses were highly leveraged.

Then Congress passed the Tax Reform Act of 1986. Liquidity immediately vanished. The dominoes began to fall. Without credit, car dealers began to close. The Savings and Loan industry fell into a black hole, and was eventually liquidated by the federal government. Many insurance companies failed.

Even before the Tax Reform Act, rental rates on property began to tumble. Developers were left with buildings they couldn't rent, mortgages they couldn't pay, and investors who refused to throw good money after bad.

The Situation

At the beginning of 1986 I had, let's say for the purpose of example, $200 of property and $150 of mortgages. Just six months later, the appraisers had reduced the value of our properties from $200 to $100. But we still had $150 in mortgages. That is not the kind of problem from which you can easily recover—if at all.

Virtually all of my competitors—at least those who used leverage like me—soon declared bankruptcy. To go bankrupt hurts, but it is not an irreparable disgrace.

Nevertheless, I sensed that God was calling me to do everything I could to avoid going bankrupt. I never sensed any promise from Him that I wouldn't have to. But I believed God wanted me to demonstrate my Christian faith to our employees, vendors, investors, lenders, family, and anyone else who might be watching.

So every day for the next seven years, I woke up not knowing whether or not I would be forced into bankruptcy.

The Feeling of Weariness

One of your greatest challenges in the middle of a meltdown is feeling weary. Some days you just wonder, "Will this ever end?"

I remember coming home for lunch one day—my regular practice. No one was there. As I stood at the sink in our darkened kitchen and looked through the window into the bright and sunny backyard, I was struck by the contrast between the darkness and the light. I said out loud, "I am so weary, I just don't know how I can go on for one more day."

> "I am so weary, I just don't know how I can go on for one more day."

Another day I had just finished a tough meeting and was walking back into my office. As I walked through the doorway,

I thought, "*That's it. I quit.*" Then I took another two steps and laughed. I thought, "*You can't quit. You hate quitters!*"

One day I was driving down a divided highway that curved in the distance. A huge bolt of lightning struck in a place that, because of the way the road curved, gave the optical illusion that it struck the middle of the road. I remember thinking, *Oh, how I wish I could have been under that bolt!*

When There's No End In Sight

Most of my troubles cleared up in about three years. But I had an institutional investor that really wanted to inflict punishment on me.

I admit in hindsight that it would have been better not to build the buildings in which they had invested (hindsight is 20-15—a little better than 20-20). But they apparently wanted me to shoulder the blame for the entire market collapse! As one writer said at the time, "Nobody is bigger than the market."

So at the five-year mark, weariness finally got the best of me. I was talking to my attorney on the phone and said, "Tommy, I just can't take it anymore. They win. I give up. Tell them they can have whatever they want."

Tommy, a great friend as well as a great lawyer, said, "Pat, I understand completely. Say, I have an idea. Why don't you just let me take the lead on this for a while, and let's see what I can do." What a relief. What a blessing from God. What an act of kindness and grace.

We All Need Some Help

I did let Tommy take the lead, and two years later—seven years after my business initially cratered—we were finally able to settle and I was spared.

Just as Joseph interpreted Pharaoh's dream, I had seven years of "great prosperity" that I squandered by going deeply in debt, followed by seven years of "severe famine" when all the abundance was forgotten (Genesis 41:26-31).

It's a long story but, by God's grace, I was able to avoid bankruptcy and not only survive, but experience extraordinary spiritual growth. I could not have done it alone. And, of course, neither can you.

In this book I want to help you. I consider it my privilege to share with you the strategies for survival and growth that worked for me then, and that can work for you now.

Why You're Going to Get Through This

Most of this book will deal with *how* you're going to get through this meltdown. But before we go there, let's talk about *why* you'll get through it.

For a Christian, the Word of God is our ultimate source of truth and strength. The Scriptures are filled with relevant texts about meltdowns. Our assurance is in the trustworthiness of God as He reveals Himself in the Bible.

> For a Christian, the Word of God is our ultimate source of truth and strength.

Here are some selected verses from the book of Isaiah in the New Living Translation. You can find the same sentiment in the other prophets, Psalms, Proverbs, and throughout the New Testament. Meditate on the character and purposes of our great God as you read, and let Him speak to your heart about the meltdown. Take your time....

> Who else knows the weight of the earth or has weighed the mountains and hills on a scale? (Yet) He picks up the whole earth as though it were a grain of sand. (Isaiah 40:12, 15)

I send good times and bad times. I, the LORD, am the
one who does these things. (Isaiah 45:7)

I will be your God throughout your lifetime—until your
hair is white with age. I made you, and I will care for you.
I will carry you along and save you. (Isaiah 46:4)

Yet for my own sake and for the honor of my name, I will
hold back my anger and not wipe you out. I have refined
you, but not as silver is refined. Rather, I have refined
you in the furnace of suffering. I will rescue you for my
sake—yes, for my own sake! I will not let my reputation
be tarnished, and I will not share my glory with idols!
(Isaiah 48:9-11)

"For a brief moment I abandoned you, but with great
compassion I will take you back. In a burst of anger I
turned my face away for a little while. But with everlasting
love I will have compassion on you," says the LORD, your
Redeemer. (Isaiah 54:7-8)

You can read other pertinent verses at Isaiah 40:23-24;
40:29-31; 43:11-13; 45:23; 49:15-16; 55:11; 56:6, and 60:10.

From start to finish, the Bible describes a God who loves
you very much. So much, in fact, that He will discipline you
for your own good (see Hebrews 12:7-11).

From these verses come two assurances.

> God is not
> sitting up
> in heaven
> wringing His
> hands about
> how this will
> all turn out.

Assurance #1

First, God is in charge. He has a plan. He
was not surprised or somehow caught off
guard by this meltdown. God is not sitting
up in heaven wringing His hands about
how this will all turn out. He is altogether
good and trustworthy. God is sovereignly

orchestrating all of the seemingly random circumstances of your life.

Assurance #2

You're going to get through this. Yes, you will have to go through it. There are no shortcuts. And, yes, you can't know how it will turn out. That belongs to the realm of God's will. And, yes, it's going to take some time. But, you will get through this.

Next, we'll talk about the greatest temptation you will have to face during the meltdown.

Questions
(for personal reflection or group discussion)

1 Are you feeling weary? Do you feel like there's no end in sight? How bad is it?

2 You may not feel like you are going to get through this, but are you willing to believe the Scriptures and put your faith in God?

3 Review Assurance #1 and Assurance #2. Do you have faith that these are true? How about your feelings? Do your feelings matter?

Two

THE TEMPTATION
TO WITHDRAW

ONE DAY AFTER I finished giving a speech, Bill wanted to speak to me privately. His cool outward demeanor was betrayed by eyes full of terror.

Bill explained that he was in the middle of an economic meltdown, and it was eating him alive.

I said to Bill, "Tell me about your devotional life. Are you reading the Bible and praying?"

He looked like I had just hit him with a cattle prod. "No," he said, "I haven't felt like doing that for some time."

Then I asked him a second question, "Do you have a best friend you can talk to? Or are you in a small group with some other men?"

"No, neither," Bill answered.

Because I work with men as a vocation, I regularly talk to men like Bill who are dealing with huge problems.

When I am with these men in public, they put on a good face. Yet, behind closed doors, knowing they are safe with me, there is often desperation, even panic, in their voices.

Can you guess one of your biggest tendencies during a meltdown? It's to withdraw from God and from friends...to go it alone...to not want others to know your struggles. It's to wear a game face that says, "Everything's okay," even though you're dying on the inside.

> Can you guess one of your biggest tendencies during a meltdown? It's to withdraw from God and from friends.

Where Did She Go?

The first time I experienced this tendency to withdraw happened soon after I became a follower of Christ.

My wife, Patsy, and I met a single woman in our church. We talked in the halls on Sunday, and frequently saw her at a large home Bible study.

Then one day she disappeared. Since we were only casual acquaintances, I didn't think much about it.

A year later, she reappeared. The story began to come out. She had been through a severe crisis. And instead of reaching out to her brothers and sisters, she had withdrawn from people and, eventually, from God.

The Two Commandments

The Bible tells us that the two most important things we can do in the whole wide world are to love God and to love people....

> Jesus replied: "'Love the Lord your God with all your heart and with all your soul and with all your mind.' This is the first and greatest commandment. And the second

is like it: 'Love your neighbor as yourself.' All the Law and the Prophets hang on these two commandments" (Matthew 22:37-40).

So where does the temptation to withdraw come from?

God is brilliant, but the devil is also quite clever. He knows that if the two most important things are to love God and love people, then tempting you to cut off God and people are his two best strategies.

Why should we be surprised, then, that the first two things we want to stop are spending time with God and people?

Besides, sometimes people give you good reasons to question whether they really love you.

"They Don't Care About Me"

During the darkest days of my economic meltdown, one of my institutional investors summoned me to a meeting. I knew if that meeting did not go well, it was over for me.

If the meeting went well, there would still be other challenges to face, but I would probably be okay. I was trusting God, but sweating bullets.

I called three of my closest friends—friends who knew the details of what I was up against—and asked them to pray.

I went to the meeting, and everything turned out just fine.

After I returned home, a week went by but none of my "closest friends" contacted me to see how the meeting went.

Ouch! That hurt.

So I called each of them and said, "I know you're very concerned about how my meeting went last week, so I wanted to call and give you the report."

Each of them said something like, "Oh yeah! I've been meaning to call you!"

Right.

At the time I thought, "They don't care about me."

But what I've since learned is that you have to give people the benefit of the doubt. Mostly they do care, but they have problems too. So you have to give them a break.

We can't expect perfect fellowship from imperfect fellows. You just never know what the other guy is going through.

Imperfect Fellowship vs. Perfect Isolation

Here's the point. If you don't feel like reading your Bible and praying, going to your small group, or being involved in your church, then that's a sure sign that these are the things you most need to do.

And if you don't have a small group or a Bible study and a church, you need to make that happen.

I know, I know. Right now you're feeling the temptation to *withdraw*, not *engage*. But engage is what you need to do. My children got tired of me saying this, but sometimes you just have to substitute discipline for a lack of natural interest.

> If you don't feel like reading your Bible and praying, going to your small group, or being involved in your church, then that's a sure sign that these are the things you most need to do.

You must decide which will most help you survive the economic meltdown—imperfect fellowship or perfect isolation.

Go ahead. If you will do what you don't want to do, you will become what you want to be. Here are three strategies to help you avoid withdrawal.

Strategy: Spend Time with God

I have two friends who share office space. They talk to each other throughout the day. But I only speak to them every two weeks or so.

As you might expect, they talk to each other in a very different way than they talk to me. That's because the degree of closeness in a relationship is proportional to the amount of time spent together.

Nothing will keep you close to God like consistent private devotions. Sometimes called "a quiet time," it's a routine period, usually at the beginning or end of the day, in which five, ten, fifteen, thirty minutes or more are set aside to read and think about God's word, pray, and possibly perform other spiritual disciplines (e.g., sometimes I write notes in a journal).

Three observations: First, a lot of people have heard of the quiet time concept but are fuzzy on the details. Second, without a quiet time, it is doubtful that you can really have a "close" personal relationship with God. Third, not many people actually have a quiet time—which means not many people have a "close" relationship with God.

> We all need a group that meets regularly, shares the same priorities, and really cares about each other.

Most people are more committed to brushing their teeth regularly than to spending time with God regularly. Doesn't make much sense, does it?

If you're not already spending time with God on a regular basis, don't blow past this strategy. If you need more information, go online for a free article, "How to Have a Consistent Quiet Time," at www.maninthemirror.org/alm/alm8.htm.

Strategy: Spend Time in a Small Group

Five popular diets were compared. The hands-down winner was Weight Watchers. Why? All the diets work, but success relies on sticking to the plan.

And why did the Weight Watchers stick with the plan? Because they have a weekly meeting to reinforce their program. So how does this apply to us? None of us can stick to our "meltdown" plan without help.

We all need a group that meets regularly, shares the same priorities, and really cares about each other. Sound too good to be true? Millions (yes, I said millions) of men and women are already doing it. And you can do it too.

Because of my small groups, I have never, ever felt alone. You don't have to be alone either.

Small groups usually study God's word together or sometimes a book like this. They pray and enjoy fellowship. You've probably been in such a group.

Personally, I have never known anyone whose life has changed in any significant way apart from the study of God's word, and usually in relationship with others.

If you want more, you can read a free article, "How to Lead a Weekly Men's Small Group," at http://www.maninthemirror. org/alm/alm94.htm

Strategy: Active Church Involvement

There is no such thing as a "Lone Ranger Christian." You can't be a Christian by yourself.

Notice the strategy is active church *involvement*, not *attendance*. I'm constantly amazed at how many people think they can be Christians without church, or *ecclesia*. The church is God's New Community—a group of people living out their faith together.

> Church is all about our vertical relationship with God and our horizontal relationship with each other.

Church is all about our vertical relationship with God and our horizontal relationship with each other. We are part of a church *vertically* so that we can worship our great God. We are part of a church *horizontally* so that we can encourage each other.

Hebrews 10:25 exhorts, "Let us not give up meeting together, as some are in the habit of doing, but let us encourage one another."

Encouragement. Let's break it down. "Courage," the root word, is "the quality or state of mind or spirit that enables one to face hardship or disaster with confidence and resolution"— that's right out of Webster.

So what does it mean to "en"-courage? To encourage is to inspire to have courage. No one needs courage to get a pay raise, have your son make the team, or move into a beautiful new home.

You need courage when you get a pay reduction, your son gets cut from the team, or you're about to lose your home.

Encouragement is the food of the heart, and every heart is a hungry heart. This is especially true in this economic meltdown. If you can't get encouragement from a church, where can you go?

If you don't have a church, you can read a free article, "How to Select a Church," at http://www.maninthemirror.org/alm/alm2.htm.

A lot of people will succumb to the temptation and withdraw from God and friends. Don't let that happen to you. Now is the time to draw close to those who love you, both God and friends.

Next let's see if we can understand how you got off track.

Questions
(for personal reflection or group discussion)

1 Are you reading the Bible and praying? Do you have a best friend you can talk to, or are you in a same gender small group? What do your answers suggest?

2 One of your biggest tendencies during a meltdown is to withdraw from God and from friends.

☐ AGREE   ☐ DISAGREE

Explain your answer.

3 Which of the three strategies to avoid withdrawal is most relevant for you, and why?

Three

UNDERSTANDING HOW YOU GOT OFF TRACK

JOHN WAS HIGHLY LEVERAGED when the stock market crashed. By Friday morning of Wall Street's worst week, John's equity was paper thin.

He said, "If the market goes down another 100 points today, they will call my margin account and I'll lose everything. On Monday morning, I'll have to start over."

As we talked on, John explained, "You know, I think I needed this. I'm only in my early 40s, but I've made so much money that I stopped working about a year ago."

The most difficult lessons to learn are often the ones we already know.

"Basically, I've been sitting around on the couch watching movies and getting fat. My life was headed nowhere. God has my undivided attention."

The most difficult lessons to learn are often the ones we already know.

Living By Your Own Ideas

Like John, during good times a lot of people get lax about doing life God's way. In fact, a lot of people have never really been trained to understand God's way.

I see this every Friday morning at The Man in the Mirror Men's Bible Study that I teach here in Orlando. Every week we have four to eight visitors. They sit at a "first timers" table with me.

Invariably, many of them have professed faith in Christ. But they want the best of both worlds. They want the benefits of Christ, but they also want to taste the good things the world has to offer. They want to have their cake and eat it too.

They read their Bibles for comfort, but *Forbes* for direction. They have been shaped more by the herds of commerce than the footsteps of Christ.

As a result, they have spent the last five, ten, fifteen or more years living by their own ideas. Their lives have not turned out the way they planned. And now they are miserable.

Biblically, these men have let the worries of this life and the deceitfulness of money choke the word and make it unfruitful (Matthew 13:22); they've let the yeast of culture work through the whole batch of dough (Galatians 5:9); they've done that which is permissible but not beneficial (1 Corinthians 6:12); and they're high risk for a great crash because they built on sand and not the rock (Matthew 7:24-27).

> Their *capabilities* are not equal to their *intentions*. As a result, they end up Christian in spirit, but secular in practice.

It's not as though these men want to struggle or fail. But their *capabilities* are not equal to their *intentions*. As Denzel

Washington, playing a recovering alcoholic, ex-military bodyguard in a Latin American country, said in *Man on Fire*, "You're either trained or you're not trained." Spiritually, most men are not. As a result, they end up Christian in spirit, but secular in practice.

So what are the root problems? There are two: *idols* and *lies.*

Idols

An idol is anything of which we say, "I *must* have this to be happy."

Every morning you go into a world that all day long tempts you to exchange the glory of God for an idol (Romans 1:23).

I race a vintage Porsche and have used racing as a platform to build relationships with men and share my faith. One day a man who never misses a chance to race asked me quite seriously, "When does my passion for racing become an idol?" Good question.

All idolatry is rooted in *unbelief.* This unbelief can take many forms, but at its root is the powerful lie, "Jesus Christ alone is not enough to make me happy. I need something else."

An idol is something we worship. The issue is looking to anything except Jesus Christ for identity, meaning, and ultimate purpose. An idol is anything that becomes the object of inordinate affection—anything that competes with our full surrender to Christ.

> Idols make promises they cannot keep, which is why you can be on a winning streak and still feel empty.

John Calvin said that men are "idol factories." Perhaps nothing interferes with our faith more than the root problem of making idols—it's the "next step" after believing a lie (more in next section).

We can make idols of almost anything, but common examples today include:

- Money
- Titles and positions (especially if the job doesn't generate a large income)
- Homes (i.e., attaching personal worth and identity to a dwelling)
- Country club memberships (i.e., being part of the "right" crowd)
- Ministry titles (e.g., elder, deacon)
- Relationships (e.g., idolizing a wife)
- Affiliations with important people
- Cars, boats, planes, motorcycles
- Our bodies (i.e., physical appearance)
- Superior intelligence
- The praise of men (what C.S. Lewis called "to win worship")
- Even our own righteousness!

All these affections are horizontal and worldly. The Bible says that all such friendship with the world is spiritual adultery (James 4:4).

Christian writer C. S. Lewis lamented how men were so easily satisfied with lesser things. Idols make promises they cannot keep, which is why you can be on a winning streak and still feel empty.

Lies

All of us either live by the truth or a *good* lie.

Every morning you go into a world where all day long you are tempted to exchange "the truth of God for a lie" (Romans 1:25).

There are two languages in the world: *truth* and *lies*.

The first language—the native tongue—of every person is the language of lies. When we receive Christ we become *bilingual.* We learn a second language—the language of truth. But what happens when we don't regularly practice speaking a second language? We revert to our native tongue.

How do we fall back into our native language? No one, Christian or otherwise, will choose to live by an obvious lie. Which counterfeit dollar bill is most likely to make it into circulation? It's the one that looks like the real thing.

In the same way, the only lies that make it into circulation are ones that appear to be true.

All of us either live by the truth or a *good* lie.

A good lie is probably only one or two degrees off course. Otherwise it would be rejected.

The problem with a good lie is that it will work—for 10, 20, even 30 years. But ultimately it will fail you, and often at the worst possible moment—like now, during an economic meltdown.

What does a good lie look like?

Two Really Good Lies

I've fallen for two really good lies in my lifetime.

Lie #1

The first lie became my worldview when I started in business: "Money will solve my problems, and success will make me happy."

I would set a goal, work really hard, six months would go by, I would meet the goal, experience euphoria, then two weeks would pass, the novelty would wear off, and I would have to do, what?

Set a new goal. And the new goal had to be, what? Bigger, brighter, better, higher, faster, sleeker, shinier, etc.

Then I would work really hard, six months would go by, I would meet the goal, experience euphoria, two weeks would pass, the novelty would wear off, and I would have to set another goal. Again, bigger, better, and so on.

The more I accomplished the more miserable I became. Money and success, it turns out, make promises they cannot keep.

Ironically, my wife, Patsy, who couldn't care less about money and success, was experiencing the love, joy, and peace I wanted.

I was committed to a set of Christian values. After all, I grew up in the church and was a moralist. But I was surprised to discover that my wife, Patsy, was committed to a personal relationship with Jesus Christ. Over time, I too embraced Christ as my Savior.

However, at that time I was a materialist, and no one told me to stop. So I was both a Christian and a materialist, which led to my second error.

Lie #2

The second lie I bought, which also became my worldview, was, "I want the best of both worlds." I wanted everything Christ had to offer, but I still wanted the best the world had to offer too.

At the ten year mark in my spiritual journey, I realized that my faith was producing a different kind of result than many of my friends.

I called a "time out" that I thought would last a couple of weeks. Instead, I spent the next two and a half years staring at my navel. One day I read Matthew 13:22:

> "The one who received the seed that fell among the thorns is the man who hears the word, but the worries of this life and the deceitfulness of wealth choke it, making it unfruitful."

I said, "That's my life." I was reading my Bible (the seed), but I had worries piled high trying to cram in as much of the world as I could. And money had choked off much of what I was reading in my Bible.

As the proverb says, "No matter how far you have travelled down a wrong road, the only solution is to turn back."

Once I realized my loyalties were divided, I surrendered and made Jesus "Lord" of my life as well as my "Savior." Of course, Jesus is always the Lord, whether we acknowledge it or not. But we can live in rebellion against Him, as I had been doing.

If applicable, do you know how you got off track?

Solving the Right Problem

What is the fundamental problem you should be trying to solve? If you don't get this right, you risk prolonging your pain.

Our nation is facing a problem of biblical proportion. As a nation, we have been living beyond our means. We have too much national debt. Many of us have too much personal debt.

As a result, most observers would say we have a financial problem. And we do.

But this "presenting" problem is really the symptom of a deeper problem.

> Fundamentally, we have a spiritual problem. It is a problem of the human heart. We have disobeyed God.

Fundamentally, we have a spiritual problem. It is a problem of the human heart. We have disobeyed God. Moses started talking about this in about 1,400 B.C. He said,

> See, I am setting before you today a blessing and a curse—the blessing if you obey the commands of the LORD your God that I am giving you today; the curse if you disobey the commands of the LORD your God and turn from the way that I command you today by following other gods, which you have not known. (Deuteronomy 11:26-28)

We see this same sentiment throughout Scripture—Old Testament and New Testament. We are told not to follow the practices of the world, adopt worldly customs, intermingle with the world, make treaties, imitate detestable ways, covet gold and silver, become engrossed with the things of this world, love money, love the world or anything in the world, or worship other gods (see Leviticus 18:3, 20:22; Exodus 34:12,16; Deuteronomy 7:2-4, 7:25, 8:19, 18:9; Joshua 23:12-13; 1 Corinthians 7:31; 1 Timothy 6:9; 1 John 2:15-16).

And what happens if we do? We become ensnared, we turn back, we do what seems right in our own eyes, we form worldly alliances that become a temptation and a trap, our hearts become stubborn, we cling to deceit, we disobey God, we exchange the truth of God for a lie, and we end up worshipping other gods.

Intermingling with the Culture

There are a lot of Scriptures that explain how people get caught up in the world. Here are two of the best:

> But they mingled with the nations and adopted their customs. They worshiped their idols, which became a snare to them. (Psalm 106:35-36)

> But people who long to be rich fall into temptation and are trapped by many foolish and harmful desires that plunge them into ruin and destruction. (1 Timothy 6:9)

You already know that you can't serve both God and money, right? But that doesn't stop us from trying, does it?

The Apostle Paul put it this way: "You were running a good race. Who cut in on you and kept you from obeying the truth?" (Galatians 5:7)

Two verses later, he answered his own question. The problem is, "A little yeast works through the whole batch of dough" (Galatians 5:9)

And that leaves us where we are today. None of us planned to be in an economic meltdown. But here we are.

One of the essential questions you need to answer is: Do you understand how you got off track?

If you are trying to solve the wrong problem, then you can only succeed by accident.

Is the problem that you have lived by your own ideas? Did you make an idol? Did you believe a lie? Did you adopt worldly customs and get ensnared?

Maybe you're an innocent bystander caught up in someone else's failings. Regardless, understanding the problem you need to solve is crucial.

If you are trying to solve the wrong problem, then you can only succeed by accident.

Next we'll look at how you can solve this problem.

Questions
(for personal reflection or group discussion)

1 To what extent have you been living by your own ideas, wanting the best of both worlds?

2 Biblically speaking, how do people get caught up in the world?

3 If applicable, do you understand how you got off track? How would you describe it?

Four

WHAT IS GOD'S PLAN FOR YOU?

MARK HAD TROUBLE SLEEPING. Over the last year, he watched his small business teeter on the brink.

Sometimes when he can't sleep, he finds himself weeping. When that happens, he repeats the words of Jesus over and over, "Come to me, all you who are weary and burdened, and I will give you rest" (Matthew 11:28). Eventually, he dozes off.

Mark said, "Sure, it's tough. But I've grown more spiritually in the last year than in the previous ten years combined. Yes, it's scary, but it's also exciting. Because I know that only God can make this right."

How God Sees You

Each week while preparing the message I teach at The Man in the Mirror Men's Bible Study, I use a worksheet to keep me on track. One of the first things I do is get my head straight on how God feels about people.

Let me summarize what the Bible has to say about you. He knit you together in your mother's womb. He knows when you sit or stand. He knows every word before it forms on the tip of your tongue. He determined the exact times and places where you would live.

When Jesus looks at you he is filled with compassion, because you are harassed and helpless, like a sheep without a shepherd. God our savior wants all men—including you—to be saved and come to a knowledge of the truth. He takes no delight in the death of the wicked.

You are his "special possession." You are the full expression of God's creative genius. God was at his very best when he made you. His love is staggering.

God's Great Desire

The first time I had a kidney stone, I was afraid I was going to die. Then, after two hours of intense pain, I was afraid I wasn't going to die!

At the Emergency Room I was begging them for some relief. Finally, they gave me a shot of morphine. Praise God!

Next, an orderly wheeled me into the bowels of the hospital to get an x-ray. My wife, Patsy, came too. When we arrived, there was a waiting line, so the orderly pushed my gurney against the wall and left.

I began talking to Patsy in a loud voice. "I feel a love for God right now like I have never felt before. I feel the presence of Jesus! I can feel the Holy Spirit coursing through my veins!"

Patsy said, "Shut up, you dummy. That's the morphine."

Of course it was. But let me ask you. Wouldn't you like to have that kind of love for God?

God's great desire is to have *a reciprocal love relationship* with you. He loves us, and the most important thing we can do is love Him with all our heart, soul, mind, and strength—the totality of our being, every ounce of our energy, and the sum of our strength. We are to bring an intensity to the loving of God.

God wants us to love him recklessly, with abandon, the way a baby squeals when daddy throws him into the air—knowing that daddy will never fail to catch him.

> God's great desire is to have *a reciprocal love relationship* with you.

"But I'm Not Good Enough"

In the middle of my meltdown, I abandoned the lie, "I can have the best of both worlds." I confessed, repented, and surrendered my life to the Lordship of Jesus.

But I had a problem. I kept having feelings of shame, guilt, and unworthiness—"I'm not good enough. I don't deserve to be rescued."

Where do you suppose those thoughts come from? That's right—the Accuser, because that's his main job, and when you're down that's his high season.

Because I listened to the Accuser, I picked up a new error: "I need to deserve grace." I began to work, work, work, hoping to make God happy (or at least avoid more of His wrath!).

As conditions worsened, I just needed some relief. I started writing out my prayers—sort of like "a psalm a day." One morning I was pouring my heart out to God. I pointed out how hard I was trying to be a godly man, a loving husband, an involved father, a man of integrity, a faithful steward, and so on.

The Lord spoke to my heart, "Pat, nothing you do will ever make you good enough for me to love you. I love you because I made you."

Wow! I had been a Christian for 14 years, but that was the first time I truly understood salvation by *grace* versus salvation by *works*. (Most of the really big ideas about Christianity take 10 to 20 years to sink in.)

Your Value to God

How about you? Are you still trying to be good enough? I know you've been beaten up, but that doesn't change how God feels about you.

Suppose I pulled my wallet out and offered you a crisp $100 bill. Would you want it? Of course you would! What if I crumpled it up into a ball—would you still want it? Of course.

> Nothing you do can ever make you good enough for God to love you. And nothing you do can ever make you bad enough for God not to love you.

What if I put it on the floor and stomped on it so it got all smudged? What if I accidentally left it in my pants pocket so it went through the laundry and bleached out? Would you still want it? Of course you would. Why? Because the condition of the bill does not alter its value.

That's how God feels about you. He doesn't like your sin, but no matter what shape your life is in, God loves you. The condition of your life doesn't alter its value to God.

Nothing you do can ever make you good enough for God to love you. And nothing you do can ever make you bad enough for God not to love you. Instead, you are good enough because He made you, and Christ died for your sins.

What God Has For You

God wants to redeem, reconcile, and restore—even prosper—you. However, He doesn't just pass this out randomly. There is a *process*, as the Israelites discovered. Jeremiah 29:10-14 says,

> This is what the LORD says: "When seventy years are completed for Babylon, I will come to you and fulfill my gracious promise to bring you back to this place. For I know the plans I have for you," declares the LORD, "plans to prosper you and not to harm you, plans to give you hope and a future. Then you will call upon me and come and pray to me, and I will listen to you. You will seek me and find me when you seek me with all your heart. I will be found by you," declares the LORD, "and will bring you back from captivity."

The Patience of God

The Bible makes it abundantly clear that God is not in any big hurry. "The Lord is not slow in keeping his promise, as some understand slowness." Why? "He is patient with you, not wanting anyone to perish, but everyone to come to repentance" (2 Peter 3:9).

Because God doesn't quickly spank us, we tend to mistake his patience for permission.

So God has a plan—it's that everyone would repent and love Him. But God is also patient. Ironically, His patience presents a problem. Because God doesn't quickly spank us, we tend to mistake His patience for permission. So what is God's plan when you've gotten off track?

The Removal of the Shakable Kingdom

God has three ways of dealing with people who believe lies and worship idols. Sometimes He withholds the thing they think they can't live without. Sometimes He gives them so much of what they want that they "gag" on it. And sometimes—as in a meltdown—he removes the thing they think they can't live without.

At the zenith of my business career, I could tell what my friends were thinking: *Wow! He must really be under God's blessing.*

But I wanted to shake them and say, "No! You don't understand. I'm gagging here. I have everything I ever wanted, and I'm miserable! I hate my life."

That led to me surrendering my life to the Lordship of Christ. God must have believed me, because I soon found myself in "the meltdown." It's as though God said, "You know, Pat, I really believe you. But you've given me so little to work with that I'm going to have to start over with you."

God leveled me to the foundation. Fortunately, I had the foundation of Christ.

The surgeon's scalpel inflicts pain, but he does it to remove the tumor that would destroy.

Then, when my economic meltdown hit, I could tell what my friends were thinking: *Wow! He must really be under God's curse!*

And, again, I wanted to shake them and say, "No! You don't understand. This is a blessing, not a curse. God is faithfully removing the shakable kingdom I built so His unshakable kingdom may remain. I've never been so happy." Here's how the writer of Hebrews put it:

> At that time his voice shook the earth, but now he has promised, "Once more I will shake not only the earth but also the heavens." The words "once more" indicate the removing of what can be shaken—that is, created

things—so that what cannot be shaken may remain. (Hebrews 12:26-27)

A Blessing or a Curse?

You may be wondering about your own circumstances, "How could losing so much be a blessing?" It's simple. You were rushing to your own destruction, and God intervened. The surgeon's scalpel inflicts pain, but he does it to remove the tumor that would destroy.

As Hebrews 12:7 says, "God disciplines us for our own good." Spiritual pundit Jamie Buckingham cleverly put it this way: "He whom God loveth, he beateth the hell out of!"

No one in their right mind would be thankful for a curse, right? Hebrews 12:28-29 says:

> Therefore, since we are receiving a kingdom that cannot be shaken, let us be thankful, and so worship God acceptably with reverence and awe, for our "God is a consuming fire."

We are exhorted to be thankful when God removes the shakable kingdom so the unshakable kingdom may remain.

God will not force you to revere Him, but He will make it impossible for you to be happy until you do.

Again, God is always committed to enjoying, or restoring, a reciprocal love relationship.

God will not force you to revere Him, but He will make it impossible for you to be happy until you do.

"It Was Good For Me To Be Afflicted"

God called King David "a man after my own heart" (Acts 14:22). God loved David.

But David became proud and sinned. Because God loved David, he afflicted David's life. He removed something David thought he could not live without. Listen to what David had to say after God melted him down.

> Before I was afflicted I went astray, but now I obey your word.... It was good for me to be afflicted so that I might learn your decrees.... I know, O LORD, that your laws are righteous, and in faithfulness you have afflicted men. (Psalm 119:67, 71, 75)

If you have been disobedient to God and He has afflicted you, it's for your own good.

So What Is God's Plan For You?

Are you an obedient person who sometimes disobeys, or have you been a disobedient person who sometimes obeys? Be honest. A lot is riding on your answer.

You may be in one of several situations.

First, you may be a Biblical Christian. You're caught up in the economic meltdown through no fault of your own.

It happens. Daniel 11:35 says, "Some of the wise will stumble, so that they may be refined, purified and made spotless until the time of the end, for it will still come at the appointed time."

Demonstrate your Christian faith to your employees/employer, vendors, creditors, investors, family, and anyone else who might be watching.

And Jesus said, "Every branch that does bear fruit he prunes so that it will be even more fruitful" (John 15:2).

Obedience is the trademark of a Biblical Christian. So continue to walk with Christ by faith, trusting that His promises are good and true.

As you do this, God will sanctify you to be even more fruitful.

What an opportunity to demonstrate your Christian faith to your employees/employer, vendors, creditors, investors, family, and anyone else who might be watching. Be sure of this, people are watching you right now to see if your faith makes any difference.

Also, you may be in the best position of all to benefit from the practical, financial, and spiritual strategies later in this book.

Second, you may be a Cultural Christian. You've made some errors in judgment. You've made a profession of faith in Christ, but you've gotten caught up in worldly ways. The greatest lesson I've ever learned is this: There is a God we want, and there is a God who is. They are not the same God. And the turning point of our lives is when we stop seeking the God we want, and start seeking the God who is.

There is a God we want, and there is a God who is. They are not the same God. And the turning point of our lives is when we stop seeking the God we want, and start seeking the God who is.

Does this make sense? God is who He is, and no amount of wanting to reinvent Him in your imagination to be the God you want is going to have one iota of impact on His unchanging nature and character.

So your task is to come humbly to the foot of the Cross and there surrender your life to the Lordship of Jesus Christ.

I suggest you do this right now. You can either pray in your own words, or this suggested prayer:

> Lord Jesus, I need You in my life right now more than I ever have. I confess that I have been worshipping other gods. I have exchanged the truth for a lie. I have been seeking the god(s) I wanted, and not the God who is. And I am sorry. I earnestly and humbly repent. I want

to have a reciprocal love relationship with You. You've done Your part. Now please show me my part. Thank You for hearing my prayer and forgiving me. I invite You to do whatever it takes for me to be in right relationship with You. I surrender all. Amen.

Third, you are a Seeker who has yet to invite Christ into your life. Frankly, an economic meltdown is a small price to pay for eternal life. In this chapter I've explained how God sees you, His great desire to have a reciprocal love relationship with you—forever, and His patience. Isn't it time for you to reach out to the One who is always reaching out to you?

> Isn't it time for you to reach out to the One who is always reaching out to you?

If you are ready to become a follower of Christ, have your sins forgiven, begin eternal life, seek the God who is, and start your process of restoration, then you can pray that in your own words, or use this suggested prayer:

Lord Jesus, I need You. I confess that I have sinned against You by worshipping other gods, and I am sorry. Thank You for dying on the Cross for my sins. By faith, I invite You to come into my life, forgive my sins, and give me the gift of eternal life. I receive You as both my Savior and Lord. I am in so much pain right now because I have lived by my own ideas. Remake me into the person You want me to be. Restore me according to Your grace and mercy. In Your Name I pray. Amen.

If you have just received Christ as your Savior and Lord, welcome to the family! You have to take personal responsibility for your life, but with Christ you now have a trustworthy guide.

Two suggestions. First, tell someone what you've done before the day is done. Second, get involved in your church or, if you're not part of a church, make finding one a priority. Don't procrastinate.

Next, let's start looking into specific practical and spiritual strategies that can help you survive the meltdown.

Questions
(for personal reflection or group discussion)

1 Is God removing "the shakable kingdom?" Why is that a blessing, not a curse? King David said, "It was good for me to be afflicted...." Are you there yet? Explain your answer.

2 Do you understand and believe that nothing you do will ever make you good enough for God to love you (or bad enough not to love you)—that He loves you because He made you and Jesus died for your sins?

3 Have you been a Biblical Christian, a Cultural Christian, or a Seeker? Did you pray and surrender your life to Christ in this chapter? What does that mean?

Five

PRACTICAL SURVIVAL STRATEGIES

BRIAN AND I WERE "Hey, it's good to see you too" friends at church.

One day Brian looked pretty down. I said, "How's it going?" as he walked by.

He said, "Not very good," and kept walking. I've learned that kind of body language and tone of voice sometimes means, "I really don't want to talk about it." But other times it means, "Gee, I wish I had somebody to talk to."

A few minutes later Brian walked back the other way. Since the only way to find out is ask, I said, "Brian, pretty bad, huh?"

"Yeah, it's pretty bad."

"Would you rather not talk about it, or would it be helpful to talk it through?"

As I had suspected, he really did want someone to reach out to him and talk it out.

Brian explained that his lawn maintenance business had dropped off sharply over the last twelve months. He wasn't sleeping, he was taking medication for depression, and his daughter cut off all contact.

He said, "I've lost hope. I just don't know what to do next." Brian was in survival mode.

What are some of the practical strategies you need just to survive? Here are the ones I found important:

- Communicate, communicate, communicate
- Cling to your integrity
- Absorb the blow
- Practice steady plodding
- Seek counsel
- Maintain a positive attitude
- Manage your private life

Let's take these one by one.

Strategy: Communication

In June 2008, one of our city's high visibility developers committed suicide. In the days that followed, the story leaked out he had embezzled an alleged $20,000,000 from his Christian partner, Hunter, and Hunter's investors.

Hunter (disguised, as are all names in this book) is as straight an arrow as they make. In fact, when the story broke, our sometimes cynical newspaper gushed about Hunter's integrity.

Still, how do you survive that kind of meltdown? Whether it's $20,000,000 or $20,000 of credit card debt, one do-or-die strategy jumps to the top of the list—communication.

Hunter didn't run and hide. Hunter didn't stop taking phone calls. Instead, he made communication one of the cornerstones of his survival strategy.

If an investor, lender, vendor, or anyone calls, Hunter takes the call. And Hunter is also proactive in communication. Every two weeks he writes an update report to his partners.

Hunter will get through this meltdown because he understands this principle: People can take bad news, but they can't stand being left in the dark.

If you're behind in a payment, can't properly service your customers, or whatever it is, the first survival strategy is to keep the lines of communication open.

Listen, I know that may be tough to swallow. But if you don't, then you give the other party no choice except to assume the worst. And assume the worst they will.

To survive you've got to communicate, communicate, communicate. I'll say more on communication in Chapter 7, "Financial Survival Strategies."

- Take your calls; don't dodge people
- Proactively communicate with customers and creditors
- Periodically report to your creditors

Strategy: Integrity

One of my most embarrassing moments came when a Savings and Loan Association that was a major tenant in one of our highest profile buildings was about to go under.

By God's grace, we had found a replacement tenant, but it was going to take a LOT of extra money to refinish the space to meet their specifications.

I approached our lender about borrowing more money. They were very reluctant, but eventually cooperated—with a stipulation. If for any reason we fell behind in debt service, I had to pledge that I would immediately—and without further comment—deed my interest in the building over to them.

So we put the new tenant in the building. Then, just as everything looked like it might be okay, the bottom fell out of the rental market. Soon, the call came. I went for a meeting and tried to persuade them to give me more time.

They said no.

I was very upset. After the meeting, I called the office and scheduled a meeting for the next morning to set up a "war room."

On my plane ride back home, option after option raced through my mind. But God wouldn't give me any peace. I tossed and turned that night.

Early the next morning I got up and thought, *I think I'll just read my Bible before I go to the office and see if God has any wisdom for me.*

I ended up in Psalm 15. It starts, "LORD, who may dwell in your sanctuary? Who may live on your holy hill?"

I thought, *Wow, that's what I'm really after. All this other stuff is lipstick and rouge.*

So I continued reading in verse two, "He whose walk is blameless and who does what is righteous, who speaks the truth from his heart and has no slander on his tongue."

> God promises that when we keep our word—even when it hurts—we will never be shaken.

That made me feel pretty good about myself. Then I came to the end of verse four and on to verse five, "who keeps his oath even when it hurts…. He who does these things will never be shaken."

Suddenly, I felt like I had been hit with a zillion gigawatts of power. I knew exactly what to do. And instantly, peace and calm swept over me.

When I arrived at the meeting, I told our team to prepare the paperwork. There would be no fight today. Yes, it was going to hurt. But God promises that when we keep our word—even when it hurts—we will never be shaken.

So, how about you? Part of your survival strategy is to keep your word—to cling to your integrity. If you do your part then, as the Scriptures promise and I can testify by my own experience, you will survive.

▸ Keep your oath even when it hurts.

Strategy: Absorb the Blow

When you get bad news, it creates the same chemical and emotional response as a near miss on the Interstate. Adrenaline pumps, and then you have a huge letdown.

"Anticipate" that you will have bad news along the way—blows. Two steps forward, one step back. When you take a blow—like a foreclosure notice or a pink slip or a customer that cancels—give yourself 24 hours to absorb the blow. Don't say anything or do anything; just walk away.

Pray about it. Pour your heart out to God about it. And then go to bed. You will feel better tomorrow. God's mercies are fresh every morning.

▸ Give yourself 24 hours to absorb any new blow.

Strategy: Practice Steady Plodding

You can only do what you can do today. And the Bible says, "A man cannot discover anything about his future" (Ecclesiastes 7:14).

If you start to worry about tomorrow, you will take on troubles you can't do anything about. Jesus put it this way: "Do not worry about tomorrow, for tomorrow will worry about itself. Each day has enough trouble of its own" (Matthew 6:34).

Instead, apply the strategy of steady plodding—make it a philosophy of life. Make your to-do-list for the day. Prioritize it. Then start chipping away. Be patient. Galatians 6:9 encourages us, "Let us not become weary in doing good, for at the proper time we will reap a harvest if we do not give up."

▸   Patiently practice steady plodding

Strategy: Seek Counsel

Since you are in an economic meltdown here are two questions you need to answer before seeking advice. First, do you really want advice? A lot of people really don't—they want support for decisions they've already made. Second, how well do you receive advice when it's offered? Can you receive advice humbly?

You need advice when you either a) think you know what to do but you're not sure, or b) you have no idea what to do.

If you think you know what to do but aren't sure, you need a voice of reason to be a reality check because many major decisions do turn out badly.

If you are at a fork in the road and honestly don't know what to do, you need someone wise who has stood at that fork before.

Proverbs 15:22 says, "Plans fail for lack of counsel, but with many advisers they succeed." If you want to be a survivor, make sure seeking counsel is one of your strategies.

Who can you call today to seek some counsel?

▸   Seek counsel from wise advisers

Strategy: Maintain a Positive Attitude

Everyone's disappointed when their world gets turned upside down—that's normal. But don't wear your feelings on your shirt sleeve. No one likes a negative sour puss walking around with a storm cloud over his head.

Here's the technology you need to maintain a positive attitude: When the phone rings and someone asks you, "How are you doing?" always answer, "Great!" (Or if that's not you, "Good!" will work—but put some enthusiasm into it.)

What if you're not "feeling" great—is it a lie to say you are? Not at all. Regardless of how you feel, your real status is "blessing," and the Bible exhorts you to "always" be joyful and thankful:

> From the fullness of his grace we have all received one blessing after another. (John 1:16)

> Rejoice in the Lord always. I will say it again: Rejoice! (Philippians 4:4)

> Be joyful always; pray continually; give thanks in all circumstances, for this is God's will for you in Christ Jesus. (1 Thessalonians 5:16-18)

Acting positively will have a Pygmalion effect on both you and those around you. In a matter of days, you can change your story from despair to joy because you trust in God. And you will attract rather than repel people.

▸ Practice a positive attitude whether you feel like it or not.

Strategy: Manage Your Private Life

Once I sold a building for one of our community's leading businessmen who had an economic meltdown.

By the time I met him, his employees were all gone. His customers were long gone. His wife had divorced him.

He had been reduced to living in his office—and it was a pigsty. Papers cluttered every available surface. Tin trays from

TV dinners were stacked around. He was disheveled and depressed.

> An alert, healthy, well-rested you is a big part of your survival strategy.

He was doing nothing to manage himself and, as a result, he wasn't surviving very well.

This may seem like a place where you can cut corners, but that is an illusion. An alert, healthy, well-rested you is a big part of your survival strategy.

Besides, no one else can take responsibility for your private life.

The list is not complicated—you already know what it is:

- ▸ Eat properly.
- ▸ Get enough sleep.
- ▸ Take regular exercise.
- ▸ Take some time off every day to recharge (maybe watch less news on TV—e.g., cut in half).
- ▸ Get away for a couple of days once a month. If you can't afford that, spend a day at the beach or similar place.
- ▸ Talk to your spouse (you've got to figure out how to not take out your frustrations here).
- ▸ Play with your children.
- ▸ Keep up with your church and other relationships.
- ▸ Practice spiritual disciplines (more in Chapter 8, "Strategies for Spiritual Growth").
- ▸ Pray with your spouse (short prayer, before work, dedicate day to God, add specific requests and thanks for answers).
- ▸ Pray with your family (e.g., grace at all meals).

Sure, you may have some problems doing these things consistently. That's life.

But you have to do the list. That's the point. Ask God to help you stay on top of your private life.

These strategies will buy you time and grace.

Questions
(for personal reflection or group discussion)

1 Where do you your circumstances need triage?

2 Which of the strategies in this chapter can help you right away, and why?

☐ Communicate, communicate, communicate
☐ Cling to your integrity
☐ Absorb the blow
☐ Practice steady plodding
☐ Seek counsel
☐ Maintain a positive attitude
☐ Manage your private life

Six

SPIRITUAL SURVIVAL STRATEGIES

WILLIAM WAS DOWNSIZED OUT of a job at the beginning of 2008. At that time he said, "I really need to get back to work. I'm a man of action, and this sitting around is getting to me."

William is a pro. He's a "getter-doner" energized by keeping busy. He identified 38 employers in his city that would be a good fit for his skills. Then he systematically connected with each company.

But William has still not found work. And now he's caught up in the larger economic meltdown. Yet his impatience to get back to work had been replaced with a quiet resolve and a spiritual peace.

William thought he had an employment problem. And, of course, he does. Yet unemployment was what God used to deepen and strengthen a personal relationship with William that, now, he wouldn't trade for anything.

Here are some proven, biblical strategies to help you find peace and strength in these times.

Don't Underestimate Prayer

Which do you think is more productive—*work* or *prayer*?

Christian writer and thinker C. S. Lewis once noted that God has given us two forms of causality: work and prayer.

First, don't *overestimate* the power of work to solve your problems. Second, don't *underestimate* the power of prayer to solve your problems.

Most people assume work is more powerful—and therefore more productive—than prayer. Why? Because when they work they see a result, but when they pray sometimes they don't.

But, as Lewis noted, because prayer is so powerful, God must put some limits on it or we would all destroy ourselves! God says we can do certain things if they are within the rules of His kingdom.

And what if we want something extra? Then he says, "Come and ask me about it, and we'll see."*

So there are two errors you want to avoid. First, don't *overestimate* the power of work to solve your problems. Second, don't *underestimate* the power of prayer to solve your problems.

▸ Don't underestimate prayer; it is more powerful than labor.

---

* C. S. Lewis, *God in the Dock,* 1970, Grand Rapids: William B. Eerdmans Publishing Company, pp. 106-107.

The Gibeonite Ruse

Scripture offers many, many examples to show how God responds when we go to him in prayer—or don't. Here's one about what happens when we don't.

When the Israelites came to conquer Canaan, the Gibeonites asked for a treaty. They showed up with moldy bread, cracked wineskins, old clothes, and claimed to come from a distant country.

Joshua 9:14 says, "The men of Israel examined their food but did not inquire of the LORD." So Joshua made a peace treaty to let them live.

Three days later, the Israelites discovered it was all a ruse! The Gibeonites lived close by. But they had given their word in the treaty. So the Gibeonites were allowed to live, but Israel made them into water carriers and woodcutters.

The Israelites looked at the moldy bread, tattered clothes, cracked wine skins, and came to the wrong conclusion. The Bible says they did this because they "did not inquire of the LORD."

> It is easy to look at the data and come to the wrong conclusion.

It is easy to look at the data and come to the wrong conclusion. This is doubly true when you are under so much financial pressure.

Let's face it. We're all tempted to rely on our own best thinking and not inquire of the Lord. Here's an example of what happens when we inquire of the Lord.

Strategy: Inquire of the Lord

To inquire of the Lord is a special form of prayer. Most of our prayers ask God to give us something we already have in mind (e.g., job, raise, move, another child). Inquiring of the Lord, however, has a different nuance. It's more about acknowledging that we really don't know what to do, and we need wisdom to understand His will.

In ancient Israel there was a famine. It lasted for three years. 2 Samuel 21:1 says,

> During the reign of David, there was a famine for three successive years; so David sought the face of the LORD. The LORD said, "It is on account of Saul and his blood-stained house; it is because he put the Gibeonites to death."

Why was there a famine? What was the problem? David didn't know. Nobody knew. So David inquired of the Lord.

He discovered that his people were being punished for something that happened in a different generation! King Saul, David's predecessor, violated the treaty made during the Gibeonite ruse and killed many of them.

Once David knew the real problem, he was able to make things right with the Gibeonites. And God stopped the famine.

▸ The ancient Israelites made a mistake because they did not inquire of the Lord.

▸ David ended a three year famine because he did inquire of the Lord.

No strategy to survive the economic meltdown is more important than "inquiring of the Lord." It's foundational.

Could it be that simple? Yes. Joshua made a treaty not to kill them, Saul killed them anyway, and David made it right. And it all revolved around inquiring—or not inquiring—of the Lord.

Obviously, there's more to surviving the meltdown than inquiring of the Lord—like taking personal responsibility and being faithful to execute. We'll look at many strategies to do just that in the pages ahead. However, no strategy to survive the economic meltdown is more important than "inquiring of the Lord." It's foundational.

▸ Inquire of the Lord about everything.

Strategy: "Letting" It Happen versus "Making" It Happen

One of your biggest battles is the desire to control or force outcomes.

At my lowest point I met with my father-in-law who is my mentor, counselor, advisor, and friend. I laid out the details of my situation, occasionally breaking down in tears.

After listening patiently for over an hour, offering empathy along the way, Dad said, "I have two things to say. First, you're going to be all right. This will work out."

My mind exploded! *Praise God! That's incredible! I didn't see any way out of this. But he's been through a lot more than me, and he thinks I'm going to make it!*

That was the plus side. Then he said, "Second, I think it will take about two years."

What? Two years? You've got to be kidding me. Why does it have to take so long?

The economic meltdown will not be quickly resolved. How long? Who knows. You can try to accelerate the process by "making" it happen, but that just won't work.

You need to hunker down. Do what you need to do—be responsible, but let it happen, and let God make it happen for you.

▸ There is a profound difference between "letting" it happen and "making" it happen.

Don't Mistake Equipping as Abandonment

Denny's business has dried up. The strain has taken a toll on his marriage. He is on medication for depression. He sees no way out. He feels forsaken—abandoned by God.

Denny couldn't feel any worse than Joseph must have felt. Joseph was sold into slavery as a teen, and sent to prison for a crime he didn't commit. But God was with him, and he rose to power in Egypt.

Some 20 years after his wicked brothers sold him, a severe famine threatened his family in Canaan. His brothers came to Joseph for food, not knowing he was still alive.

They were terrified to learn Joseph had so much power. But Joseph said, "Do not be distressed and do not be angry with yourselves for selling me here, because it was to save lives that God sent me ahead of you.... You intended to harm me, but God intended it for good...." (Genesis 45:5, 50:20).

What appeared to be abandonment was equipping.

What appeared to be abandonment was equipping.

After 400 years of slavery in Egypt, Moses had a vision that he was going to rescue his people. But when he killed an Egyptian, he was forced to flee to the wilderness for 40 years. Then God appeared in a burning bush and sent Moses to fulfill the vision he had so many years before.

After 40 years, I'll bet Moses knew that wilderness pretty well. What appeared to be abandonment was equipping.

God equips us to be even more fruitful (John 15:2). But once you surrender to Christ, he will never, ever abandon you:

> Keep your lives free from the love of money and be content with what you have, because God has said, "Never will I leave you; never will I forsake you." (Hebrews 13:5)

God has not abandoned you. Jesus said, "I give them eternal life, and they will never perish. No one can snatch them away from me." (John 10:28)

Distinguish between equipping and abandonment—knowing they feel about the same.

Strategy: Give It Time

Twenty years for Joseph. Forty years for Moses.

Don't try to force things. It's less than 300 miles from the Nile to Jerusalem, yet it took Moses and the Israelites 40 years to make the journey. Why was that?

The Israelites had been living by their own ideas. They made idols and worshipped other gods (the first and second of the Ten Commandments, Deuteronomy 5:7-8). Their hearts turned back toward Egypt. So God disciplined them. He used those 40 years to work some things into and out of their character.

God has a plan. I could have tried to "make" my problems go away faster, but at what cost? Like the wandering Israelites, God wanted to work some things "into" and "out of" my character—and yours too.

In fact, I suggest you not even ask God to shorten the duration of your hard times. The Israelites tried to no avail. Instead, ask God to ensure you learn everything He has for you during this hard time. If you artificially shorten the hard times without learning everything God has for you, then you will (probably) have to travel this road again.

It's going to take some time. Let it happen. Are you trying to force it?

Strategy: Proverbs 3:25-26 for Fear

In August 1981 the prime interest rate hit an all-time high of 20.5%. One thing is for sure. In 1981, you didn't want your loans tied to prime!

Unfortunately, mine were—commercial real estate loans. Frankly, I was dumb to have them at all, but what could I do at that point? It was a little late. Noah built the ark before it rained.

At the time I was a baby Christian. I had a genuine "saving" faith. But it wasn't a seasoned "living" faith.

There was no question in my mind the Bible was true. But my faith was small and weak. I didn't have enough experience with God in hard times to have faith that He would get me through.

And I was a nervous wreck. I was about to buckle.

One morning I read Proverbs 3:25-26:

> Have no fear of sudden disaster or of the ruin that overtakes the wicked, for the LORD will be your confidence and will keep your foot from being snared.

Wow! I read and reread that passage. Then I memorized it. Over and over again, I kept repeating those words.

God used His word to calm me down, increase my faith and, ultimately, to keep my foot from being snared.

Today, my faith is a "populated" faith—I have many experiences I can point to when God kept my foot from being snared.

What is your experience with God? If you are a seasoned veteran, then you already know the power of God's word. If you are a new or baby Christian, let Proverbs 3:25-26 and other verses of Scripture calm you.

▶ Have no fear of sudden disaster or ruin, the Lord will keep your foot from being snared.

What do we do when our circumstances are difficult? Steady plodding, day by day, in faith and obedience, not taking matters into our own hands, constantly inquiring of the Lord and letting it happen versus making it happen.

Now let's turn our attention to some financial strategies.

Questions
(for personal reflection or group discussion)

1 What has been your experience with prayer? Why should inquiring of the Lord be a key strategy right now?

2 What is the difference between "letting" it happen and "making" it happen? Which do you practice most often, and what changes do you need to make?

3 Does fear sometimes overwhelm you? How can Proverbs 3:25-26 or another favorite verse keep you on an even keel?

Seven

FINANCIAL SURVIVAL STRATEGIES

THERE IS NO PAIN quite like cash flow pain, is there? Depending on how severely the economic meltdown has affected you personally, here are some financial strategies to help you survive.

Strategy: Get Out of Debt

Here's an idea that often gets overlooked: It takes more energy to earn a living and service debt than to just earn a living.

Debt is dumb. If you are in debt, getting out of debt is "do-or-die."

My strategy for overcoming debt was simple. First, I made "getting out of debt" my overarching goal. For seven years that was my #1 business priority. I knew that to survive, I had to get out of debt. So do you.

Second, I told everyone with whom I did business, "I am pledging all of my business assets to all of my business debts."

There was a complication—one that might be difficult to understand unless you have a business background. I had business assets and business debts, and I had personal assets but no personal debt. Like a fool, I had "personally guaranteed" my business debts. In other words, I offered my personal assets (e.g., home) to cover my business debts in case my business assets were insufficient.

> It takes more energy to earn a living and service debt than to just earn a living.

The "pledge" strategy worked—probably because I didn't have any lavish personal assets like expensive paintings, jewelry, or second homes.

The idea that I was willing to pledge all my business assets, as it turned out, gave everyone with whom I did business a good bit of relief and confidence to work with me. Give it a try.

Third, I told everyone, "I promise that I will treat everyone exactly the same." I agreed to give no one preferential treatment as we divvied up my business assets. Again, a great confidence builder. Of course, you have to deliver on the promise!

So, to summarize, my debt strategy was:

▸ To make getting out of debt my overarching goal.
▸ To pledge all of my business assets to all of my business debts.
▸ To promise that I would treat all my creditors equally.

These three strategies stabilized my situation—step one. These same strategies, or some derivative, can probably stabilize your situation too.

In a hospital Emergency Room, the first step is to stabilize the patient, the second step is to correct the problem (e.g., surgery), and the final step is rehabilitation. You've just read about how to stabilize. Now let's look at strategies to correct the problem.

Strategy: Accessibility

I quickly discovered that the people who do "work outs" for borrowers think very differently than the people who made the loans!

Basically, they believe no one, trust no one, and assume you are always lying all the time. Why? Because with most customers it's true! Their customers tend to dodge calls, not return calls, not do what they promise, and miss deadlines.

This creates a fantastic opportunity for you to distinguish yourself and get some mercy.

Here are some strategies to try for both debt and overdue payments. First, for your initial contact, proactively meet with your creditors to explain your circumstances and propose a plan—always in person if possible. A phone call is a distant second for the first contact, and mail is a non-starter. As a wise man once said, "Go. If you can't go, call. If you can't call, write."

Second, if someone you owe money to tries to make contact, you must always take their call or return their call as soon as possible—let's call this the strategy of "accessibility."

And, third, if a creditor sends you email or snail mail, pick up the phone and give them a call. They will be blown away! It's all about keeping or restoring trust.

Fourth, don't wait for your creditors to call you. Call them periodically and give them an update if you feel up to it. Or you may want to send them a written monthly update (always include your contact information so they can easily get hold of you if they need a clarification).

The accessibility strategies are:

- To proactively meet with creditors in person
- To always take your creditors calls
- To respond to creditor mail by picking up the phone
- To update your creditors regularly

I didn't say it's easy. I hated it. My ego was already bruised, and it was embarrassing. Yet, it's a key strategy to make it through. Why? Because so few others will do it.

Motivate yourself with the axiom I mentioned earlier: Sometimes you have to substitute discipline for a lack of natural interest.

Strategy: Always Do What You Say

Speaking of keeping or restoring trust, here's another axiom: All disappointment is the result of unmet expectations.

Every time you make a promise, your creditor writes that down. Did you know that? They keep a written record. And when you don't keep your promise their expectation is unmet. Hence, disappointment. It's tough to placate someone who is disappointed in you.

So, first of all, don't make promises you already know you can't keep—that's obvious.

Second, when you make a promise, you have to keep it. Do what you say you will do. Now, here's the problem. Your circumstances may be changing, even deteriorating, rapidly. Can't keep the promise after all?

Third, if you can't keep a promise, pick up the phone and tell them.

Most people are already so depressed in a meltdown, that when their circumstances take another blow, the last thing they "feel" like doing is picking up the phone. So, substitute discipline for a lack of natural interest. It works. Give it a try.

The strategies to help you always do what you say are:

- To not make promises you know you can't keep

- ▸ To keep the promises you do make
- ▸ To proactively revise any promise you find you can't keep

Strategy: Shed Personal Liabilities

If you own a business or properties, you have no doubt struggled with "personal liability" on borrowing for business assets.

I read in Proverbs 22:26-27 one day:

> Do not be a man who strikes hands in pledge or puts up security for debts; if you lack the means to pay, your very bed will be snatched from under you.

In response, I vowed never to give personal liability on a building or business loan. Then one day, the perfect deal came along, but the only way it would work is if I signed personally on the mortgage note. I did.

After that, I signed personally on a regular basis. For the next seven years it was a great run—until Congress passed the Tax Reform Act of 1986.

Once you cross the line you said you'd never cross, it's very easy to keep going further and further down that road. I rationalized Proverbs 22:26-27. I thought, *It says "if" I lack the means to pay. That seems pretty unlikely. These assets are very valuable.* And then, suddenly, they were worth half as much.

I was talking to my attorney on the phone one day and said, "I just can't believe that I was so stupid that I signed all these notes with personal guarantees."

If you are in debt with personal guarantees, the Bible gives some very specific advice about what to do:

> My son, if you have put up security for your neighbor, if
> you have struck hands in pledge for another, if you have
> been trapped by what you said, ensnared by the words
> of your mouth, then do this, my son, to free yourself,
> since you have fallen into your neighbor's hands: Go and
> humble yourself; press your plea with your neighbor!
> Allow no sleep to your eyes, no slumber to your eyelids.
> Free yourself, like a gazelle from the hand of the hunter,
> like a bird from the snare of the fowler. (Proverbs 6:1-5)

This is the text that led me to make "getting out of debt" my
overarching goal. I did exactly what the passage suggests, and
it took seven years. But, oh, what a day that was to become
debt free!

The strategy is:

‣ Do whatever it takes to get out of personal guarantees

Strategy: Live "Within" Your Means

People either live "above" their means, "at" their means,
"within" their means, or "below" their means.

If you've been living "above" or "at" your means, then this
is your opportunity to get loose from the snare of materialism
and worldliness.

In times like these, the wise cut back.

How? The first step is to get out of *denial* that you are *not*
living within your means. Frankly, denial is a much stronger
force than most people understand. There are appearances to
keep up. Denial means that you actually believe a story that
you've made up—a lie.

The second step is to *repent*. The Apostle Paul wrote, and I
feel the same way:

> Even if I caused you sorrow by my letter, I do not regret
> it. Though I did regret it—I see that my letter hurt you,
> but only for a little while—yet now I am happy, not

because you were made sorry, but because your sorrow led you to repentance. For you became sorrowful as God intended and so were not harmed in any way by us. Godly sorrow brings repentance that leads to salvation and leaves no regret, but worldly sorrow brings death. (2 Corinthians 7:8-10)

The third step is to *grieve* what could have been. You will no doubt be filled with shame, guilt, regret, anger, and many other emotions. Let them out—preferably with an understanding spouse or same gender friend.

Fourth, don't be a *victim*. Be a victor. God is big enough to work it out. This is a matter of faith and attitude.

Finally, make a *budget* that you can afford. If you have to move in with your parents for a season, so be it. Pay off your debts—start with the ones that carry the highest interest rates. If you can't figure this out on your own, see a financial counselor. Take a Crown Financial Ministries course (www.crown.org). If you must, see a bankruptcy lawyer (as I said earlier, it's not an irreparable disgrace).

Oh, and one more thing. If it's possible, you may want to consider living "below" your means. Why would you want to do that? First, for your children—so they don't grow up materialistic and suffer financial dysfunction. Second, for God's kingdom—because you don't want to be distracted by life's worries, riches, and pleasures (Luke 8:14). And you don't want to be engrossed by the things of this world (1 Corinthians 7:30-31). And you recognize that the world and its desire pass away, but the one who does the will of God lives forever (1 John 2:17).

The steps to live within your means are:

> ▸ Get out of denial that you're overspending
> ▸ Repent for being materialistic and worldly

▸ Grieve what could have been
▸ Don't be a victim
▸ Prayerfully consider living "below" your means.

In Chapter 10, "Your Personal Action Plan," you'll have an opportunity to process the 16 bullet points from this chapter.

Questions
(for personal reflection or group discussion)

1 How much of a problem is debt for you? Which of the points about debt resonated with you the most, and why?

2 Is it easy or difficult for you to remain accessible? Explain.

3 Are you living above, at, within, or below your means? How did that happen? What do you need to do?

Eight

STRATEGIES FOR
SPIRITUAL GROWTH

A S SAID EARLIER, GOD'S great desire is for a reciprocal love relationship with you—for you to live in vital communion with the living Christ.

To accomplish this, He wants to change the core affections of your heart—that's the starting point. And then He wants you to grow in spiritual maturity—to be transformed, to renew your mind, to heal your relationships, and to give you the desire and power to do His will.

You already know you can't do this on your own, right? That's because our sinful nature resists God. Galatians 5:17 says:

> For the sinful nature desires what is contrary to the Spirit, and the Spirit what is contrary to the sinful nature. They are in conflict with each other, so that you do not do what you want.

Strategy: Live by the Spirit

A man said, "I feel like there are two dogs inside me fighting."
A friend asked, "Which one is winning?"
"The one I feed the most," he answered.
There is a solution. Galatians 5:16 puts it this way:

> So I say, live by the Spirit, and you will not gratify the
> desires of the sinful nature.

God has not left us alone. Jesus sent the Holy Spirit to
comfort, counsel, convict, convert, sanctify, and sustain us.
The strategy is:

▸ Live by the Spirit.

To "live by the Spirit" is part of a "cluster" of concepts that all
bring about this reciprocal love relationship and vital communion. The cluster includes living by the Spirit, the surrendered
life, heart transformation, and living in the overflow.

Strategy: "Daily" Surrender

To live by the Spirit is to lead a surrendered life. In Chapter
Four, "What Is God's Plan For You?" I invited you to pray a
prayer of surrender if you had found yourself off track. I hope
you did surrender your life to the
Lordship of Jesus. That was a seminal
decision.

*Jesus is the
perfect example of
a surrendered life.*

But because we are in a battle
against our "old sinful nature," there
is also a sense in which you and I
must *each day* surrender to the Lordship of Jesus and live by
the Spirit.

What does a surrendered life look like? The simple answer
is Jesus—Jesus is the perfect example of a surrendered life.

The story is told about an elementary school class that went to the studio of a famous sculptor. As the children entered they had to pass by the statue of a very ferocious and realistic lion.

One of the students said, "Hey mister, how were you able to make such a realistic looking lion?"

He answered, "Son, it was easy. I took a large block of marble, and then I simply chipped away everything that didn't look like a lion."

In the same way, you are like a large block of marble. So how can you lead a surrendered life? Simply bring yourself into the presence of God, and invite the Holy Spirit to chip away everything that doesn't look like Jesus.

When God brought me to my senses, I realized that I had tried to change the unchanging God into the God I wanted. It never occurred to me that God wanted to change me.

Because I am a rebel—as most of us are—I realized that I must *each day* come humbly to the foot of the Cross and surrender to the Lordship of Jesus.

Daily surrender, Lordship, live by the Spirit. That's the deal:

- ▸ Let the Spirit chip away everything that doesn't look like Jesus
- ▸ Surrender daily to the Lordship of Jesus

The irony of surrender is that it leads not to defeat but victory.

By the way, here are my two favorite verses to help me get in the surrendered mode:

> Search me, O God, and know my heart; test me and know my anxious thoughts. See if there is any offensive way in me, and lead me in the way everlasting. (Psalm 139:23-24)

> Who can discern his errors? Forgive my hidden faults. Keep your servant also from willful sins; may they not rule over me. Then will I be blameless, innocent of great transgression. (Psalm 19:12-13)

Strategy: Become a Disciple

Every week at our Bible study I meet men who "profess" faith but haven't been discipled to "possess" faith.

Evangelism without discipleship is cruel.

Christianity is about *heart transformation,* not *behavior modification.* That's why God wants to change the core affections of your heart. "Heart" in Hebrew is *lab* and includes your *intellect, will,* and *emotions*—everything.

How is your heart transformed? First and foremost are the strategies already mentioned—to live by the Spirit and lead a surrendered life. But you also have to "renew your mind"— or get discipled. Romans 12:2 says,

> Do not conform any longer to the pattern of this world, but be transformed by the renewing of your mind. Then you will be able to test and approve what God's will is—his good, pleasing and perfect will.

A disciple is *called* to walk "with" Christ (evangelism), *equipped* to live "like" Christ (learning), and *sent* to live "for" Christ (service, neighbor love).

The "learning" part of discipleship comes by practicing the spiritual disciplines.

Strategy: The Spiritual Disciplines

The spiritual disciplines are God's ordained means to make disciples. They help us live by the Spirit, lead a surrendered life, experience heart transformation, and live in the overflow of your relationship with Jesus.

Christian authors have been writing on spiritual disciplines since biblical times. In my book *A Man's Guide to the Spiritual Disciplines* I include the disciplines of *creation, the Bible, prayer, worship, the Sabbath, fellowship, counsel, fasting, spiritual warfare, stewardship, service,* and *evangelism.* And there are many more.

> The spiritual disciplines are God's ordained means to make disciples.

Spiritual disciplines help you continue Monday through Saturday what you begin on Sunday. They are habits to help you cultivate a daily walk.

Actually, spiritual disciplines do not "effect" change, nor do they earn any merit or improve your record with God. But they do put us into the real presence of the Holy Spirit with a surrendered, teachable heart.

Spiritual disciplines help you please God, lead a peaceable life, be a godly spouse, raise godly children, and demonstrate to the world that there really is a difference.

Which ones should you pursue? Here are the essential minimums for you during the economic meltdown and, of course, beyond:

- ‣ Reading the Bible
- ‣ Prayer
- ‣ Worship
- ‣ Sabbath observance
- ‣ Fellowship
- ‣ Counsel
- ‣ Stewardship
- ‣ Evangelism

Detailing these disciplines is beyond the scope of this book, so I would encourage you to talk to your pastor, read a book, get your small group to do a book study on the spiritual disciplines, or go online for these free articles and messages (addressed to men, but applicable to all):

> Spiritual disciplines help you continue Monday through Saturday what you begin on Sunday.

- ▸ "How to Have a Consistent Quiet Time"
  www.maninthemirror.org/alm/alm8.htm

- ▸ "The Five Defining Disciplines of Growing Men"
  www.maninthemirror.org/alm/alm14.htm

- ▸ "A Man's Guide to the Spiritual Disciplines"
  www.maninthemirror.org/alm/alm145.htm

- ▸ "Six Habits of Spiritually Happy Men"
  www.maninthemirror.org/alm/alm122.htm

- ▸ Find over 450 articles to help you grow at:
  www.maninthemirror.org/alm/index.htm and
  www.maninthemirror.org/weeklybriefing/index.htm

- ▸ Find 350 Bible study messages for podcasting or video
  download at www.maninthemirror.org/biblestudy/
  series.htm

And what if you don't feel like practicing spiritual disciplines? Honestly, there are days when I would rather check my email than read my Bible and talk to God. Sometimes I feel like skipping church.

So what's the solution? First, remember that you have a very real adversary who would consider it a victory to get you to withdraw from God.

If that doesn't jolt you into action, then you must go into a quiet wood and stay there until you hear His voice, see His face, feel the warmth of His embrace, and feel the salty taste of repentant tears running down your face.

You can't be a Biblical Christian if your capabilities don't equal your intentions.

Remember, you need the spiritual disciplines. They're crucial. You can't be a Biblical Christian if your capabilities don't equal your intentions.

A Typical Week: How It Was

It's Sunday morning, and you're exhausted from a brutal week. You're running on the fumes from last Sunday's message and worship. This day, the pastor preaches a scintillating sermon. The music lifts you into the presence of God. You walk out of church a new person—full of Jesus.

On Monday, you have an especially grueling meeting that seems like it will never end. By the end of Monday you are down to three quarters of a tank. By Tuesday afternoon, the pressure of too many bills and not enough customers starts to get to you. You're down to half a tank. The rest of the week is equally draining.

By Saturday morning, you only have one eighth of a tank left. You and your spouse spend the day in "divide and conquer" mode. You shuttle between soccer games and piano recitals. Dusk finally comes, and you fall asleep watching TV.

It's Sunday morning again. You're exhausted from a brutal week, again. Your gauge shows empty and, once again, you're running on the fumes of last Sunday's message and worship.

You rouse your family and get ready for church. You pile in the car. You're already on "E" and half way to church you start to sputter. Fortunately, you crest the brow of a hill and can see your church below in the distance. Your engine dies, but you have enough momentum to coast into the parking lot.

You shuffle, exhausted, into the sanctuary and find your regular seats. You plop down in your chair, cross your arms, and think, *Okay, pastor. I'm here. We made it—barely. This meltdown is killing me. I really need to hear from God today. So go ahead. Amaze me.*

And the pastor does amaze! The worship is awesome. You walk out of church a new person—full of Jesus. On Monday, you have an especially grueling meeting, etc., etc.

And so it goes. You are living out of the reserves of your relationship with Jesus. You don't really have enough Jesus for yourself, much less enough to share with others who are also hurting.

There is a better way. It's living in the overflow of a "daily" relationship with Christ. How can you live in this overflow of a daily walk with Christ?

- ▸ Live by the Spirit
- ▸ Daily surrender
- ▸ Become a disciple
- ▸ Practice the "spiritual disciplines."

In this next chapter, let's look at how everything mentioned might work together so you can have a "daily walk" instead of a "weekly fix."

Questions
(for personal reflection or group discussion)

1 What concepts are in the "cluster" that leads to the reciprocal love relationship and communion that God desires? Are you living out of the reserves of your relationship with Jesus?

2 What is a disciple (as described in this chapter), and how do you become one?

3 What has been your experience with spiritual disciplines? Which ones need your attention now?

Nine

PUTTING IT ALL TOGETHER: A TYPICAL WEEK

Sunday

It's Sunday morning. Today is going to be a day of Sabbath observance. God has made it legal for you to take a day of rest.

You lay in bed for a few extra minutes. Your mind calls up the faces of friends, coworkers, and people from church. You know the circumstances of some, but not others. You pray for them all, trusting the Holy Spirit brought them to mind for a reason.

Having slept soundly and feeling rested and alert, you marshal your family off to church. You prepared for worship today by praying, and as you walk into the sanctuary you sense God's presence.

> God has made it legal for you to take a day of rest.

Since you know that Christianity is expressed horizontally as well as vertically, your antenna is up for someone who looks like they could use a word of encouragement—a hungry heart.

You're surprised at your newfound sensitivity for other people who are struggling. You can't believe you hadn't noticed all the body language before.

During the offering you think, *How odd. When I was making more money I didn't feel like I could afford to tithe, but now that I'm making less money I feel like I can't afford not to tithe.*

After lunch and after playing catch with your son, you find your way to your favorite chair for some "think time" about the sermon.

You realize you've always resisted getting plugged in and becoming discipled. You now realize that's how you got off track. You thought money would solve your problems, that success would make you happy, and that you could have the best of both worlds. No more!

You realize you were a Cultural Christian who sought the God you wanted. You repented, and fully surrendered your life to the Lordship of Jesus Christ. You are so grateful for God's patience, which you had mistaken for permission.

> Now what you're after is a reciprocal love relationship and vital communion with the living Lord.

Now what you're after is a reciprocal love relationship and vital communion with the living Lord. You are so thankful that God is removing the shakable kingdom. It may look to others like a curse, but you know it's a blessing. You know that God has good plans for you—the pastor just said so!

You get a good night's rest. In fact, that has become your regular practice. You realize you need to take care of your private life—rest, diet, and exercise.

Monday

Before the family stirs, you pick up *The One Year Bible* you recently purchased and spend fifteen minutes reading the day's entry and praying over the day. This has become your regular practice five days a week.

Next, you have many challenges ahead of you this week, so you write them all down. The size of the list overwhelms you with fear. You look up Proverbs 3:25-26 and claim it for your life. Once the fear subsides, you inquire of the Lord about what to do—like an ongoing conversation between two friends who spend a lot of time together.

When you finished reading this book, you and your spouse worked through "Your Personal Action Plan" together (next chapter). You pull it out now, and review the "who does what by when" list to see what needs attention this week. And then, it's off to work.

About 10:00 a.m., a long time customer calls and presses you to make a promise you know you can't keep. You are afraid you might make them mad. You resist, and tell them what you can promise. Thankfully, they accept it.

After dinner, which you now always eat with your family, you and your spouse talk through each other's days— which you now do every day.

Monday proved to be a pretty good day. You went to the YMCA during lunch and had a good workout. The afternoon is quiet, so you conserve energy and go home an hour early to beat rush hour traffic.

After dinner, which you now always eat with your family, you and your spouse talk through each other's days—which you now do every day.

You watch a rented movie to recharge and get to bed early. Tomorrow's a big day.

Tuesday

Today you skip personal devotions, because Tuesday morning starts with the small group you recently joined.

You had to fight against the tendency to withdraw from God and people, but now you are happy you pushed through those feelings. These men are becoming your brothers.

Today, the leader starts out by describing the feeling of weariness. Then he shares several Bible verses, and finishes with the assurances that God is in control, and that you will get through this.

You take comfort that millions of others are also meeting in similar small groups. The fellowship makes you feel like these men care about you personally. Their heartfelt prayers really strengthen you.

You're off to work, and have a great morning.

Tuesday afternoon you take two calls from vendors to practice the strategy of "accessibility" and write a monthly report to your investors. You also initiate a call to a creditor about a bill you just received in the mail.

Today, you implement the decision to be a better witness to your family. You start by praying before you eat dinner. After dinner you play in the backyard with your kids.

Wednesday

On Wednesday morning during your quiet time with God, you read verses about the importance of scrupulous integrity.

For lunch on Wednesday, you meet for counsel with a Christian businessman from your small group. This started because you made a comment about how weary you are. He then asked you, "Would you rather talk about it, or not talk about it?" You said, "Yes."

Your problem is that you have so many fires on so many fronts that you don't know which ones to fight. He tells you,

"You're in crisis mode. Your focus needs to be on stabilizing your situation."

Together, you agree that rebuilding sales, improving efficiencies to cut costs, and restructuring your debt are the main priorities.

> You take comfort that millions of others are also meeting in similar small groups.

He asks you, "Do you have someone who can take the lead for a while? I think it would help you recharge."

That evening you talk to your spouse about taking a weekend break—an overnighter to the beach. Together, you pray for wisdom. When you realize you can't really afford it, you decide to make it a day at the beach. You're good with that.

Thursday

Thursday's Bible reading declares that God owns everything, and that His ways are not our ways.

As you read, the Holy Spirit quickens thoughts to your mind. You now realize debt is dumb.

Actually, you always knew debt is dumb, but the most difficult lessons to learn are the ones you already know.

This thought drives you to introspection. You realize that you were living by your own ideas. The worries of this life had choked the Word. The yeast of culture had worked its way through the whole batch of dough.

You want to rebuild your life on the rock. You know that to pull this off, you will have to start living "within" or "below" your means.

Your spouse gets up, and you share what you've been thinking. You agree to set aside a couple of hours Saturday afternoon to work on a family budget that will stop the bleeding.

Midmorning Thursday you get a "setback" call. A big deal you were counting on falls through. Your first impulse is to feel a sense of panic. *I've got to make something happen.* Instead, you pull out a copy of Assurance #1 and Assurance #2 and read them.

The strategy of "letting" it happen versus "making" it happen isn't easy, but you know it's the only way to go, if you want to stay sane.

> The strategy of "letting" it happen versus "making" it happen isn't easy, but you know it's the only way to go.

You realize you will have to break some promises, but that can wait until tomorrow. For today, you know that you need time to absorb the blow. God's mercies are fresh every morning.

For the rest of the day, you concentrate on keeping a positive attitude even though you are feeling pretty puny.

Friday

While reading your Bible on Friday morning, you are astounded by God's promises to answer prayer. You realize that you've grossly underestimated the power of prayer and inquiring of the Lord.

When you arrive at work, you get busy and call the people you promised based on the big deal that fell through yesterday. That takes most of the morning.

During the morning, you notice a co-worker who seems down. While you didn't mix business with personal in the past, now it seems so natural to you. You say, "You seem a little down. What's the matter?"

You learn her husband has been laid off and can't find work. She says, "He has no friends—nobody that really cares about him." You volunteer to have breakfast with him one day next week. She brightens for the rest of the day. Interestingly, your spirits are lifted too.

You've expected a large payment from a customer "any day now" all week long. On the strength of your customer's assurance to pay, you promised your primary supplier a payment "no later than the close of business Friday."

You're happy to see the payment arrive. You cut a check to your supplier and, to keep your promise, hand-deliver the check personally. The supplier is pleased, and the two of you have a pleasant visit about the unpleasant economy.

While you didn't mix business with personal in the past, now it seems so natural to you.

Friday night is date night! You and your spouse catch the early bird at your favorite restaurant—they're having a "buy one, get one free" entrée promotion.

It's early to bed. You can't wait to meet with God early Saturday morning to see what He has for you.

Saturday

Your eyes pop open. You don't need an alarm clock—you're like a little kid on Christmas. You've wanted to read the story of Joseph for some time, and this is the day.

You're blown away by God's Master Plan—that He would go to such extremes to provide for His people. You're equally blown away at how much pain God allowed Joseph to endure to put him in the right place at the right time. You certainly understand how Joseph could have mistaken equipping for abandonment—because you've been there!

You realize that in the same way you once mistook God's patience for permission, you now have mistaken God's equipping as abandonment. You are humbled.

When you see how long it took for Joseph to be restored, you realize your restoration may take some time. But you're okay with that, because God is in control.

Your budget meeting with your spouse after lunch has some spirited discussion, but you both agree to make getting out of debt your overarching goal. You prioritize your debts based on which ones have the highest interest rates. Also, you decide to move heaven and earth to get out of the personal guarantees you made on two business loans. You're determined to live within your means.

You're determined to live within your means.

You enjoy a wonderful family dinner and, after watching some TV, head off to bed early, eager to start all over again Sunday morning.

As you're about to doze off, you think, *You know, tomorrow I'm going to ask my pastor to help me figure out how I can start serving the Lord.*

Questions
(for personal reflection or group discussion)

1 What part of the story did you most identify with?

2 Which strategy in the story is your strong suit?

3 Which strategy needs more attention, and what should you do?

Ten

YOUR PERSONAL ACTION PLAN

THE VALUE OF THIS book will increase sharply if you turn some of these strategies into a Personal Action Plan.

Read this chapter with a pencil. Mark it up. If you see something you want to do, check it off—not too much though. Isolate the "do-or-die" issues for you and focus on them. Mark them boldly so you can't miss them. Once you check off an item, write down "the next right step" and "who does what by when"—that will help you keep it real.

1. You're Going to Get Through This

Strategy: God's Word.

- ☐ When you're down, reread the Bible verses in Chapter One, and other verses throughout the book.
- ☐ As an act of your will, put your faith in the trustworthiness of God and His Word, not your feelings.

Strategy: For Facing Bankruptcy.

☐ If you are facing bankruptcy, see a trained professional immediately.

Strategy: Someone to Take the Lead.

☐ Is there someone like "Tommy" who can take the lead for a while?

Strategy: Two Assurances.

☐ Photocopy or cut out Assurance #1 and Assurance #2 and review them daily. After a few days you'll probably stop noticing them, so move them once a week or so.

2. Triage: The Temptation to Withdraw

Strategy: Don't Withdraw.

☐ Resist the temptation to withdraw. Instead, engage. It's better to have imperfect fellowship than perfect isolation.

Strategy: Time With God.

☐ Spend "quiet" time with God for 15 minutes a day. Read a chapter of the Bible. Pray for your needs and the needs of others. Praise and thank God for His promises and provisions. Surrender your day and life to His will.

Strategy: Small Group.

☐ Spend time in a small group. Are you currently in a small group? If so, are you being transparent with them, and why or why not? If not in a group, start or join one. Or if your current group is too shallow, find a new group. If you don't know how, ask your pastor for help.

Strategy: Church.

- ☐ Be actively involved in church—vertically with God through worship and the preaching of God's word, and horizontally with people by not withdrawing from them and by offering words of encouragement to others.

3. Understanding How You Got Off Track

Strategy: Idols.

- ☐ What is your idol(s), and are you prepared to dispose of it?

Strategy: Lies.

- ☐ What is the lie or lies you have believed (e.g., "Money will solve my problems, and success will make me happy," or "I can have the best of both worlds")? And are you prepared to exchange the lie for the truth of God?

Strategy: Understand How You Got Off Track.

- ☐ Do you understand how you got off track?
- ☐ Describe how you got off track in writing—no more than one page.

4. What Is God's Plan for You?

Strategy: God's Love.

- ☐ You get that it is God's great desire to have a reciprocal love relationship with you.
- ☐ You understand and believe that nothing you do will ever make you good enough for God to love you (or bad enough not to love you)—that He loves you because He made you and Jesus died for your sins.
- ☐ Write out your prayers if so inclined.

Strategy: The Shakable Kingdom.

- ☐ God is removing the shakable kingdom so that His unshakable kingdom may remain. I get it.
- ☐ You will ponder this and Hebrews 12:28-29 until you can say with King David, "It was good for me to be afflicted" (Psalm 119: 67, 71, 75).

Strategy: Biblical Christian.

- ☐ You are a Biblical Christian caught up in the economic meltdown through no fault of your own. Claim Daniel 11:35 and John 15:2 as truths.

Strategy: Cultural Christian.

- ☐ You have been a Cultural Christian who sought the God you wanted rather than the God who is. You have surrendered your life to the Lordship of Jesus by praying the prayer (or similar) in this book. If you didn't pray earlier but would like to now, here is the suggested prayer:

> Lord Jesus, I need You in my life right now more than I ever have. I confess that I have been worshipping other gods. I have exchanged the truth for a lie. I have been seeking the god(s) I wanted, and not the God who is. And I am sorry. I earnestly and humbly repent. I want to have a reciprocal love relationship with You. You've done Your part. Now please show me my part. Thank You for hearing my prayer and forgiving me. I invite you to do whatever it takes for me to be in right relationship with You. I surrender all. Amen.

Strategy: Seeker.

☐ You have been a Seeker and have prayed the prayer in this book (or similar) for Jesus to forgive your sins and, by faith, come into your life as Savior and Lord. If you didn't pray to receive Christ earlier, here's the prayer again whenever you're ready:

> Lord Jesus, I need You. I confess that I have sinned against You by worshipping other gods, and I am sorry. Thank You for dying on the Cross for my sins. By faith, I invite You to come into my life, forgive my sins, and give me the gift of eternal life. I receive You as both my Savior and Lord. I am in so much pain right now because I have lived by my own ideas. Remake me into the person You want me to be. Restore me according to Your grace and mercy. In Your name I pray. Amen.

☐ You have told someone that you have received Christ as your Savior and Lord.

☐ You have become involved in your church, or found a church where you will become active.

5. Practical Survival Strategies

Strategy: Communication.

☐ Take your calls, don't dodge people.

☐ Proactively communicate with creditors.

☐ Periodically report to your creditors.

Strategy: Integrity.

☐ Write every area where you have compromised, or considered compromising, your integrity. What can you do to immediately change your direction?

☐ You commit to keep your oath even when it hurts.

Strategy: Absorb the Blow.

☐ Give yourself 24 hours to absorb any new blow.

Strategy: Steady Plodding.

☐ Patiently practice steady plodding.

Strategy: Seek Counsel.

☐ Seek counsel from wise advisers.
☐ Talk to a qualified friend about your situation.
☐ Who can you call today to seek some counsel?

Strategy: Maintain a Positive Attitude.

☐ Practice a positive attitude whether you feel like it or not.

Strategy: Manage Your Private Life.

☐ Eat properly.
☐ Get enough sleep.
☐ Take regular exercise.
☐ Take some time off every day to recharge (maybe watch less news on TV—e.g., cut in half).
☐ Get away for a couple of days once a month. If you can't afford that, spend a day at the beach or similar.
☐ Talk to your spouse (figure out how to not take your frustrations out here).
☐ Play with your children.
☐ Keep up with your church and other relationships.
☐ Practice spiritual disciplines (more in the chapter "Strategies for Spiritual Growth").
☐ Pray with your spouse (short prayer, before work, dedicate day to God, add specific requests, thank for answers).
☐ Pray with your family (e.g., grace at all meals).

6. Spiritual Survival Strategies

Strategy: Prayer.

- ☐ Don't underestimate prayer; it is more powerful than labor.
- ☐ It is easy to look at the data and come to the wrong conclusion—as the Israelites discovered with the Gibeonites.
- ☐ Inquire of the Lord about everything. No strategy to survive the economic meltdown is more important than "inquiring of the Lord." It's foundational.

Strategy: "Letting" It Happen versus "Making" It Happen.

- ☐ There is a profound difference between "letting" it happen and "making" it happen. Where are you trying to force it?
- ☐ Are you mentally and emotionally prepared that this may take some time?
- ☐ Don't mistake equipping as abandonment—knowing they feel about the same.

Strategy: For Fear.

- ☐ Have no fear of sudden disaster or ruin, the Lord will keep your foot from being snared.
- ☐ Memorize Proverbs 3:25-26.

7. Financial Survival Strategies

Strategy: Get Out of Debt.

- ☐ Make getting out of debt your overarching goal.
- ☐ Pledge all of your business assets to all of your business debts.
- ☐ Promise that you will treat all your creditors equally.

Strategy: Accessibility.

- ☐ Proactively meet with creditors in person.
- ☐ Always take your creditors' calls.
- ☐ Respond to mail by picking up the phone.
- ☐ Update your creditors regularly.

Strategy: Always Do What You Say.

- ☐ Don't make promises you know you can't keep.
- ☐ Keep the promises you do make.
- ☐ Proactively revise any promise you find you can't keep.

Strategy: Shed Personal Liabilities.

- ☐ Do whatever it takes to get out of personal guarantees.

Strategy: Live "Within" Your Means.

- ☐ Are you living above, at, within, or below your means? What do you need to do?
- ☐ Get out of denial that you're overspending.
- ☐ Repent for being materialistic and worldly.
- ☐ Grieve what could have been.
- ☐ Don't be a victim.
- ☐ Prayerfully consider living "below" your means.

8. Strategies for Spiritual Growth

Strategy: Live by the Spirit.

- ☐ You understand there is a battle.
- ☐ You understand living by the Spirit is how you win your battle.
- ☐ You understand how to live by the Spirit. If not, you can read a free article, "How to Walk in the Spirit," at www.maninthemirror.org/alm/alm11.htm.

Strategy: "Daily" Surrender.

- ☐ Let the Spirit chip away everything that doesn't look like Jesus.
- ☐ Surrender daily to the Lordship of Jesus.

Strategy: Become a Disciple.

- ☐ To "renew your mind" you must become a trained disciple.
- ☐ You understand what a disciple is. If not, you can read a free article, "What Is a Disciple, and How Do You Make One?" at www.maninthemirror.org/alm/alm107. htm.

Strategy: The Spiritual Disciplines.

- ☐ You understand that the spiritual disciplines are how you train to be a disciple.
- ☐ The essential disciplines for the meltdown that you are practicing include:
  - ☐ Reading the Bible
  - ☐ Prayer
  - ☐ Worship
  - ☐ Sabbath observance
  - ☐ Fellowship
  - ☐ Counsel
  - ☐ Stewardship
  - ☐ Evangelism

AFTERWORD

I T HAS BEEN MY honor to share these strategies with you. As you turn back to your own set of circumstances, may God deliver you sooner rather than later. And may we not soon forget the lessons learned. Please don't blow off the Personal Action Plan. Pick five to ten major strategies and work them into your routines. Consider forming a group to discuss the questions at the end of each chapter. An hour a week per chapter would suffice.

And to reiterate, if you want to reach out with this message to your friends, neighbors, or co-workers, we're setting up a website, www.survivethemeltdown.org, with tons of FREE resources to help you—videos, video clips, a small group leader's guide, articles, and helpful links. And if you want to present, or have someone present, a seminar, speech, or sermon to your church or business group, you will find downloadable message transcripts, sermon ideas, speaker notes, listener outlines, graphics, and sample promotional materials. We're also offering special pricing to buy books in bulk. You can arrange for a Man in the Mirror faculty to teach a seminar, or purchase a Meltdown Outreach Event Planning Kit. You can even leave a comment!

Let me conclude by restating the two Assurances from Chapter One. First, God is in control. He has a plan. He was not caught off guard by this, and He is not wringing His hands about how it's all going to turn out. He is sovereignly orchestrating all of the seemingly random circumstances of your life. Second, you will get through this. You have to be patient— you just never know what God is doing. It will take some time, but you will get through this. I am praying for you.

Seeking answers to get through these tough financial times?

Equip your congregation to survive the economic meltdown…

1 Give everyone in your church a copy of **How to Survive the Economic Meltdown** by Patrick Morley.

2 Host a 2-hour **Surviving the Economic Meltdown** outreach event.

Bulk pricing for boxes of 16 and 60 books. The more you buy, the more you save!

Try This! Preach a sermon or sermon series on How to Survive the Economic Meltdown (we'll even supply the sermon outlines if you want!).

Try This! Get your congregation to study the book in small groups and develop their own Personal Action Plans.

BOOKS!
by the box
Great Christian titles up to 85% off

For more information, call (800) 929-2536, or go to www.survivethemeltdown.org.

This 2-hour outreach will draw your community into your building and give them an opportunity to come to Christ.

- **You Teach It:** You will receive everything you need to lead the event yourself.

- **Faculty Led:** A nationally-known speaker will lead your event.

- **Business Event:** Host a one-hour presentation at a breakfast or luncheon.

To schedule an event or more information, contact Pam Adkins, at (800) 929-2536 or pamadkins@maninthemirror.org.

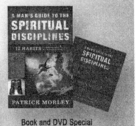

Arm Yourself

Finally, a men's devotional magazine for men who are willing to dream big, think big and risk big.

"I have been receiving *Equipping the Man in the Mirror* since its inception and LOVE IT. Over the past year, I have ordered 50 copies per printing and give them out to men in my church. Many have told me they read it everyday and they look forward to the next edition. My small accountability group discusses a topic from it just about weekly when we meet. I see more and more men monthly start to use the devotionals. The magazine is POWERFUL!"

— T.P., Kentucky

Subscribe today at www.maninthemirror.org

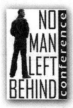

Imagine a Revolution...

a Revolution of Generosity.

www.GenerousGiving.org

Encouragement, tools and
stories to grow in your
journey of generosity.

Smart Christian Giving℠ begins at
www.nationalchristian.com

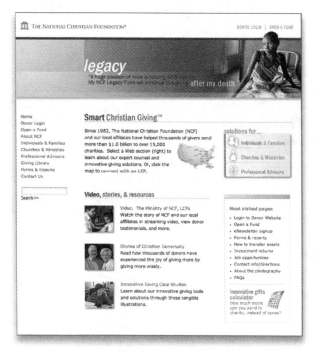

Since 1982, The National Christian Foundation and our network of local Affiliates has helped thousands of individuals and families give over $1.8 billion to churches and ministries worldwide.

Learn more about our innovative giving solutions and explore how you can give more creatively and easily at **www.nationalchristian.com**, or call **800.681.6223**.

THE NATIONAL
CHRISTIAN
FOUNDATION®

Notes

Notes

Notes